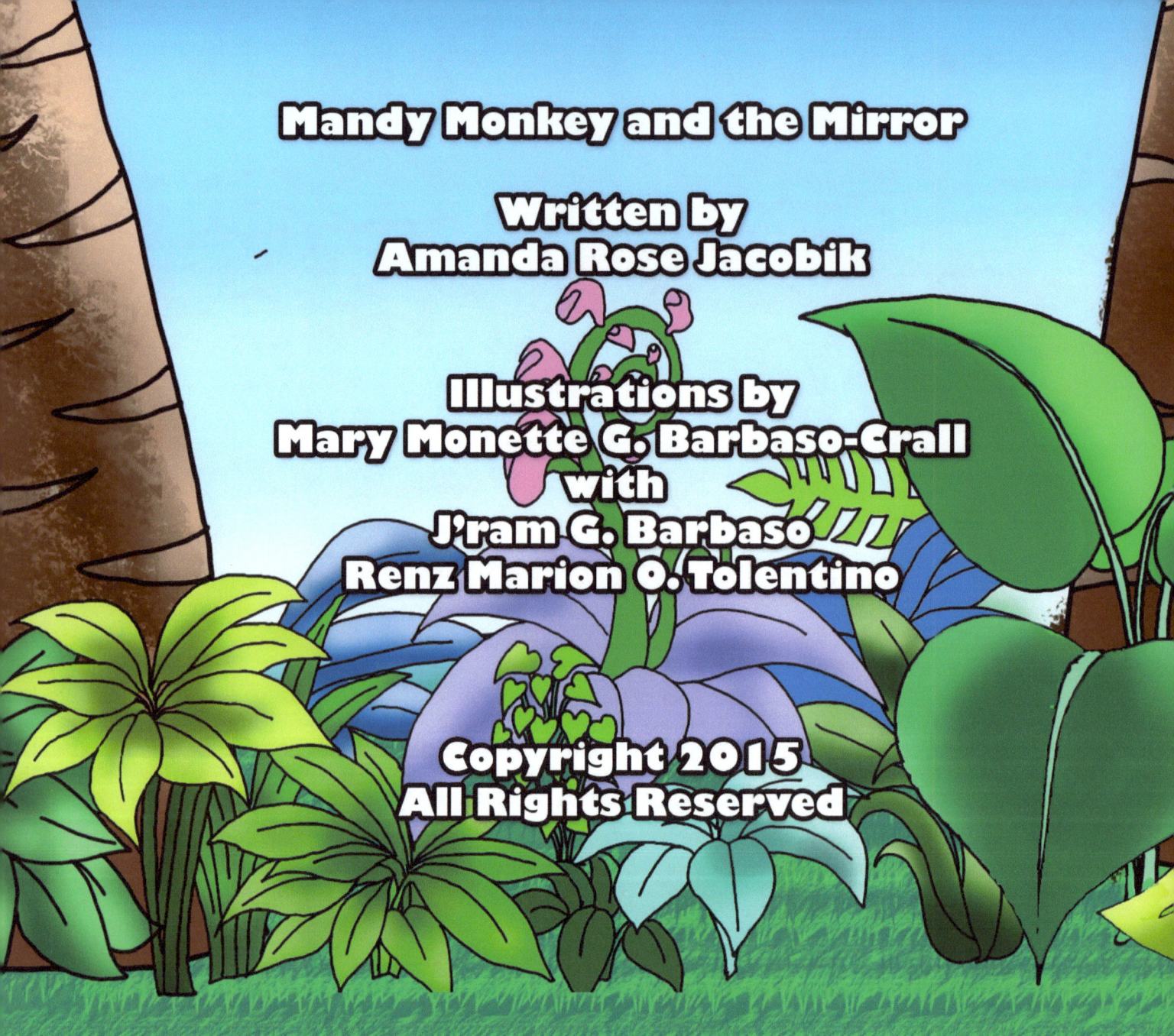

Mandy Monkey and the Mirror

Written by
Amanda Rose Jacobik

Illustrations by
Mary Monette G. Barbaso-Crall
with
J'ram G. Barbaso
Renz Marion O. Tolentino

Copyright 2015
All Rights Reserved

Any reproduction of this material without proper permission from the author is strictly prohibited by law.

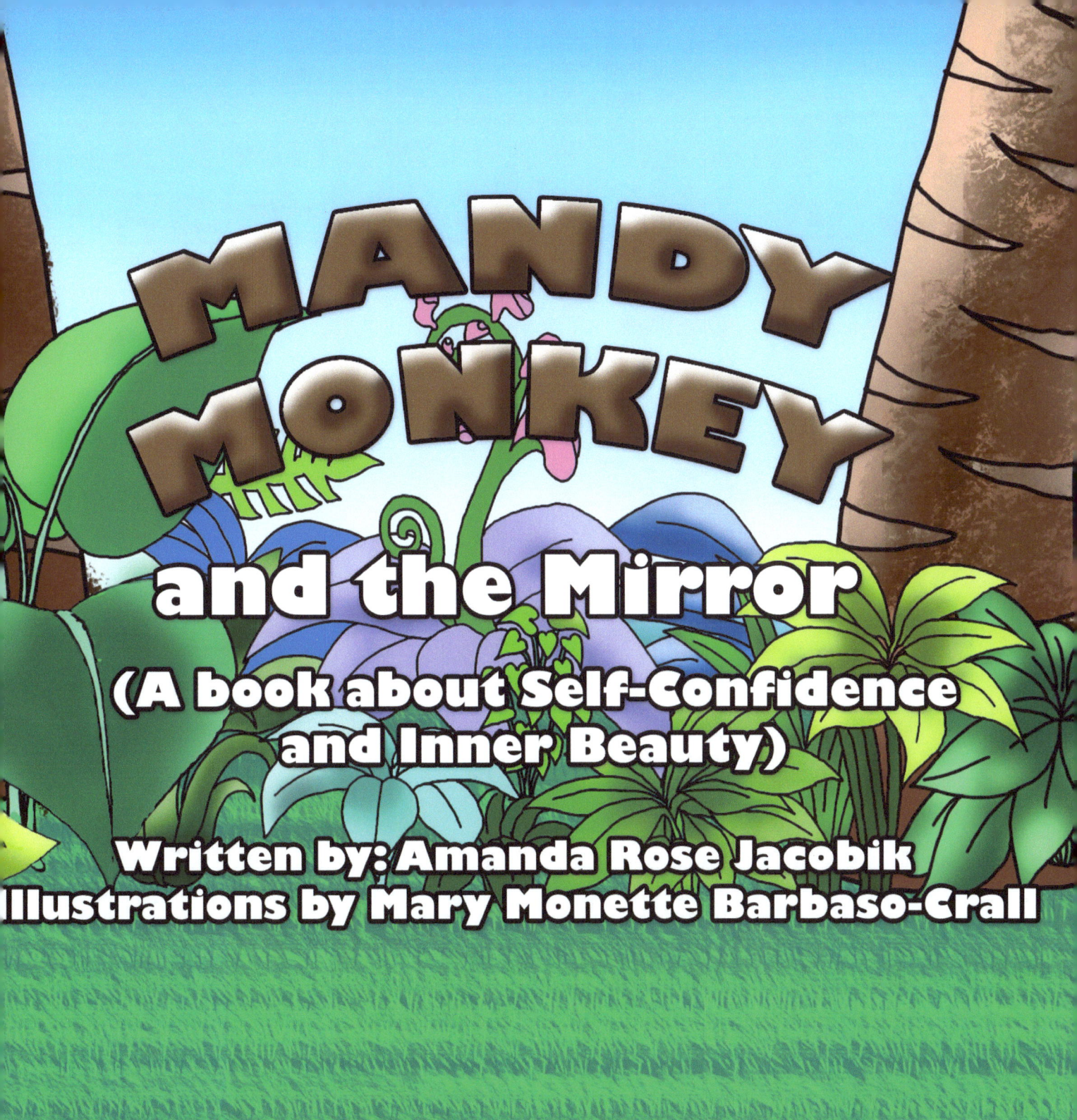

DEDICATION

To my loving Memere, Rosemarie Kalin, for being one of my strongest supporters and caretakers. You were constantly there in my time of need while regaining my health. Your support and love allowed me to grow into the young woman I am today.

Much Love... Amanda

Mandy is embarrassed about her small size. She gets teased by her friends, Georgia Giraffe, Ella Elephant, and even Farrah Flamingo. They all laugh at her from time to time.

She wished her ears were a little bigger like Ella Elephant's. Ella always got compliments on their size; she could hear all the animals gossiping all the way across the bay!

Mandy was always jealous of Georgia Giraffe. She was tall and everyone went to her for help to get mangos off trees with her long and lean legs; she didn't have to climb all the way up the tree like Mandy.

Farrah Flamingo was the one who has always stood out from the rest though. She has feathers so bright that even the sun beams off of them like fireworks! There is never a feather out of place. Farrah is always so neat and poised!

Mandy would do everything possible to try to look like her friends. She tried wearing earrings so her ears would look a tenth as good as Ella's.

She tried wearing taller shoes so her friends would start paying attention and would ask Mandy for her help with tasks like they did with Georgia Giraffe.

Mandy even tried brightly colored bows and brushed her fur a lot more so she could look half as pretty as Farrah and more grown up.

"There is so much more to you than just the outside Mandy," Georgia said. "You have more energy than anyone I know! I've never seen anyone climb up a tree as fast as you. It's impossible not to have fun around you Mandy!"

Mandy realized her friends were right; she was all those things they said. Once Mandy could see this she was able to finally just be herself, because she was beautiful in every way.

www.ingramcontent.com/pod-product-compliance
Lightning Source LLC
Chambersburg PA
CBHW041233040426
42444CB00002B/148